WISE QUOTES: PYTHAGORAS

(150 PYTHAGORAS QUOTES)

Rowan Stevens

A blow from your friend is better than a kiss from your enemy.

A fool is known by his speech; and a wise man by silence.

A good Soul hath neither too great joy, nor too great sorrow: for it rejoiceth in goodness; and it sorroweth in wickedness. By the means whereof, when it beholdeth all things, and seeth the good and bad so mingled together, it can neither rejoice greatly; nor be grieved with over much sorrow.

A man is never as big as when he is on his knees to help a child.

A stone is frozen music.

A stranger, if just, is not only to be preferred before a countryman, but a kinsman.

A thought is an idea in transit.

Ability and necessity dwell near each other.

Above all have respect for yourself.

Above the cloud with its shadow is the star with its light.

Abstain from animals.

Alas, what wickedness to swallow flesh into our own flesh, to fatten our greedy bodies by cramming in other bodies, to have one living creature fed by the death of another!

Allow not sleep to close your eyes before three times reflecting on Your actions of the day. What deeds Done well, what not, what left undone?

Anger begins in folly, and ends in repentance.

Animals share with us the privilege of having a soul.

As long as man continues to be the ruthless destroyer of lower living beings he will never know health or peace. For as long as men massacre animals, they will kill each other.

As soon as laws are necessary for men, they are no longer fit for freedom.

As soon as you awake, in order Lay the actions to be done the coming day.

As the sea-crab swimmeth always against the stream, so doth wit always against wisdom.

Assist a man in raising a burden; but do not assist him in laying it down.

Astonishing! Everything is intelligent!

Be silent or let thy words be worth more than silence.

Before all, be real. Only the truth gives to the word the Orpheus' Lyre power.

Begin thus from the first act, and proceed; and, in conclusion, at the ill which thou hast done, be troubled, and rejoice for the good.

Better be mute, than dispute with the Ignorant.

Bless us, divine number, who generated gods and men. Number contains the root and source of eternally flowing creation.

But respect yourself most of all.

Choose always the way that seems the best, however rough it may be; custom will soon render it easy and agreeable.

Choose rather to be strong of soul than strong of body.

Concern should drive us into action and not into a depression. No man is free who cannot control himself.

Consider before acting, to avoid foolishness: It is the worthless man who speaks and acts thoughtlessly.

Dear youths, I warn you cherish peace divine, and in your hearts lay deep these words of mine.

Declining from the public ways, walk in unfrequented paths.

Despise all those things which when liberated from the body you will not want; invoke the Gods to become your helpers.

Disbelieve nothing wonderful concerning the gods, nor concerning divine dogmas.

Do not despise anyone: an atom shadowing.

Do not even think of doing what ought not to be done.

Do not go to bed until you have gone over the day three times in your mind. What wrong did I do? What good did I accomplish? What did I forget to do?

Do not say a little in many words but a great deal in a few.

Do not spend in excess like one who is careless of what is good, nor be miserly; the mean is best in every case.

Do not talk a little on many subjects, but much on a few.

Don't eat your heart.

Don't try to cover your mistakes with false words. Rather, correct your mistakes with examination.

Each celestial body, in fact each and every atom, produces a particular sound on account of its movement, its rhythm or vibration. All these sounds and vibrations form a universal harmony in which each element, while having it's own function and character, contributes to the whole.

Educate the children and it won't be necessary to punish the men.

Envy has been, is, and shall be, the destruction of many. What is there, that Envy hath not defamed, or Malice left undefiled? Truly, no good thing.

Every man has been made by God in order to acquire knowledge and contemplate.

Evolution is the Law of Life Number is the Law of the Universe Unity is the Law of God

Friends are as companions on a journey, who ought to aid each other to persevere in the road to a happier life.

Friends share all things.

Friendship is one soul in two bodies.

Geometry is knowledge of the eternally existent.

God built the universe on numbers.

Golden Verses So-called because they are "good as gold." They are by some attributed to Epicarmos, and by others to Empedocles, but always go under the name of Pythagoras, and seem quite in accordance with the excellent precepts of that philosopher. They are as follows: Ne'er suffer sleep thine eyes to close Before thy mind hath run O'er every act, and thought, and word, From dawn to set of sun; For wrong take shame, but grateful feel If just thy course hath been; Such effort day by day renewed Will ward thy soul from sin. E. C. B.

Govern your tongue before all other things, following the gods.

Government exists only for the good of the governed.

Hate and fear breed a poison in the blood, which if continued, affects eyes, ears, nose and the organs of digestion. Therefore, it is not wise to hear and remember the unkind things others might say about you.

Having departed from your house, turn not back; for the furies will be your attendants.

He buries gold who hides the truth.

He is not rich, that enjoyeth not his own goods.

He who knoweth not what he ought to know, is a brute beast among men; he that knoweth no more than he hath need of, is a man among brute beasts; and he that knoweth all that may be known, is as a God among men.

I would have to say the probability of us dying seems extremely high.

If men with fleshly mortals must be fed, and chew with bleeding teeth the breathing bread; what else is this but to devour our guests, and barbarously renew Cyclopean feasts? While Earth not only can your needs supply, but, lavish of her store, provides for luxury; a guiltless feast administers with ease, and without blood is prodigal to please.

If there be light, then there is darkness; if cold, heat; if height, depth; if solid, fluid; if hard, soft; if rough, smooth; if calm, tempest; if prosperity, adversity; if life, death.

If you have a wounded heart, touch it as little as you would an injured eye. There are only two remedies for the suffering of the soul: hope and patience.

If you're asked: What is the silence? Respond: It is the first stone of the Wisdom's temple.

In anger we should refrain both from speech and action.

In this theater of man's life, it is reserved only for God and angels to be lookers-on.

Instruct thyself for time and patience favor all.

It is better to be silent, than to dispute with the Ignorant.

It is better wither to be silent, or to say things of more value than silence. Sooner throw a pearl at hazard than an idle or useless word; and do not say a little in many words, but a great deal in a few.

It is difficult to walk at one and the same time many paths of life.

It is only necessary to make war with five things; with the maladies of the body, the ignorances of the mind, with the passions of the body, with the seditions of the city and the discords of families.

It is required to find the infinitely big inside what's infinitely small to feel the presence of God.

It is requisite to defend those who are unjustly accused of having acted injuriously, but to praise those who excel in a certain good.

Know that death comes to everyone, and that wealth will sometimes be acquired, sometimes lost. Whatever griefs mortals suffer by divine chance, whatever destiny you have, endure it and do not complain. But it is right to improve it as much as you can, and remember this: Fate does not give very many of these griefs to good people.

Know thyself and thou wilt know the universe.

Learn silence. With the quiet serenity of a meditative mind, listen, absorb, transcribe, and transform.

Let a man use great reverence and manners to himself.

Let exercise alternate with rest.

Let no one persuade you by word or deed to do or say whatever is not best for you.

Let not sleep fall upon thy eyes till thou has thrice reviewed the transactions of the past day. Where have I turned aside from rectitude? What have I been doing? What have I left undone, which I ought to have done?

Love that shines from within cannot be darkened by obstacles of the world of consequences!

Lust weakens both body and mind.

Man know thyself; then thou shalt know the Universe and God.

Many words befall men, mean and noble alike; do not be astonished by them, nor allow yourself to be constrained.

Meditate upon my counsels; love them; follow them; To the divine virtues will they know how to lead thee. I swear it by the One who in our hearts engraved the sacred Tetrad, symbol immense and pure, Source of Nature and model of the Gods.

Most men and women, by birth or nature, lack the means to advance in wealth or power, but all have the ability to advance in knowledge.

Music is the harmonization of opposites; the conciliation of warring elements.

Neither will the horse be adjudged to be generous, that is sumptuously adorned, but the horse whose nature is illustrious; nor is the man worthy who possesses great wealth, but he whose soul is generous.

No man is free who cannot control himself.

No one is free who has not obtained the empire of himself.

None but God is wise.

None can be free who is a slave to, and ruled by, his passions.

Number is the ruler of forms and ideas, and the cause of gods and demons.

Numbers have a way of taking a man by the hand and leading him down the path of reason.

Numbers rule the universe.

Oh, my fellow men, do not defile your bodies with sinful foods. We have corn, we have apples bending down the branches with their weight, and grapes swelling on the vines. There are sweet-flavored herbs, and vegetables which can be cooked and softened over the fire, nor are you denied milk or thyme-scented honey. The earth affords a lavish supply of riches, of innocent foods, and offers you banquets that involve no bloodshed or slaughter; only beasts satisfy their hunger with flesh, and not even all of those, because horses, cattle, and sheep live on grass.

One must choose in all things a mean just and good.

Power is the near neighbor of necessity.

Practice justice in word and deed, and do not get in the habit of acting thoughtlessly about anything.

Practice restraint over the following: appetite, first, as well as sleep, lust, and anger.

Reason is immortal, all else mortal.

Remind yourself that all men assert that wisdom is the greatest good, but that there are few who strenuously seek out that greatest good.

Respect gods before demigods, heroes before men, and first among men your parents; but respect yourself most of all.

Respect yourself... The rest will follow.

Rest satisfied with doing well, and leave others to talk of you as they will.

Salt is born of the purest parents: the sun and the sea.

Silence is better than unmeaning words.

So in life, some enter the services of fame and others money, but the best choice is that of those few who spend their time in the contemplation of nature, and as lovers of wisdom.

So tutor youth that the sins of age be not imputed to thee.

Some are slaves of ambition or money, but others are interested in understanding life itself. These give themselves the name of philosophers, and they value the contemplation and discovery of nature beyond all other pursuits.

Souls never die, but always on quitting one abode pass to another. All things change, nothing perishes. The soul passes hither and thither, occupying now this body, now that... As a wax is stamped with certain figures, then melted, then stamped anew with others, yet it is always the same wax. So, the Soul being always the same, yet wears at different times different forms.

Speak not nor act before thou hast reflected.

Step not beyond the beam of the balance.

Strength of mind rests in sobriety; for this keeps your reason unclouded by passion.

The animals share with us the privilege of having a soul Alas, what wickedness to swallow flesh into our own flesh, to fatten our greedy bodies by cramming in other bodies, to have one living creature fed by the death of another! In the midst of such wealth as earth, the best of mothers, provides, yet nothing satisfies you, but to behave like the Cyclopes, inflicting sorry wounds with cruel teeth! You cannot appease the hungry cravings of your wicked, gluttonous stomachs except by destroying some other life.

The beginning of every government starts with the education of our youth.

The earth affords a lavish supply of richness of innocent foods, and offers you banquets that involve no bloodshed or slaughter; only beasts satisfy their hunger with flesh, and not even all of those, because horses, cattle, and sheep live on grass.

The experience of life in a finite, limited body is specifically for the purpose of discovering and manifesting supernatural existence.

The highest goal of music is to connect one's soul to their Divine Nature, not entertainment.

The most momentous thing in human life is the art of winning the soul to good or evil.

The octave formed a circle and gave our noble earth its form.

The oldest, shortest words - 'yes' and 'no' - are those which require the most thought.

The soul of man is divided into three parts, intelligence, reason, and passion. Intelligence and passion are possessed by other animals, but reason by man alone.

!

The stars in the heavens sing a music, if only we had ears to hear.

The wind is blowing. Adore the wind.

The wise man should be prepared for everything that does not lie within his control.

There are men and gods, and beings like Pythagoras.

There is a good principle which created order, light, and man, and an evil principle which created chaos, darkness, and woman.

There is geometry in the humming of the strings, there is music in the spacing of the spheres.

There is no word or action but has its echo in Eternity.

Those alone are dear to Divinity who are hostile to injustice.

Thou shalt likewise know that according to Law, the nature of this universe is in all things a like.

Thought is an Idea in transit, which when once released, never can be lured back, nor the spoken word recalled.

Time is the soul of this world.

To cognize the Divine Essence — this is the highest purpose of soul, sent by the Creator to the Earth!

Truth is so great a perfection, that if God would render himself visible to men, he would choose light for his body and truth for his soul

Truth is to be sought with a mind purified from the passions of the body. Having overcome evil things, thou shalt experience the union of the union mortal divinity with the mortal man.

We come from God. As the tree from the root and the stream from the spring; that's why we should always be in contact with Him, as the trunk from the root. Because the stream dries up when it is separated from the spring and the tree dies when is uprooted.

We ought not to quit our post without the permission of Him who commands; the post of man is life.

We ought so to behave to one another as to avoid making enemies of our friends, and at the same time to make friends of our enemies.

Wealth is a weak anchor, and glory cannot support a man; this is the law of God, that virtue only is firm, and cannot be shaken by a tempest.

When going to the temple to adore Divinity neither say nor do anything in the interim pertaining to the common affairs of life.

When the wise man opens his mouth, the beauties of his soul present themselves to the view, like the statues in a temple.

Wind indeed increases fire, but custom love.

Wisdom, thoroughly learned, will never be forgotten.

Without Justice, no realm may prosper.

Write in the sand the flaws of your friend.

You should help a man to take up a burden, but you should not help him put it back down.

You should make great things, not promising great things.

You will know that wretched men are the cause of their own suffering, who neither see nor hear the good that is near them, and few are the ones who know how to secure release from their troubles.

www.ingramcontent.com/pod-product-compliance
Lightning Source LLC
Chambersburg PA
CBHW071256070526
44583CB00017B/2493